The Stick Soldiers
by
Hugh Martin

Winner, 2012 A. Poulin, Jr. Poetry Prize
Selected by Cornelius Eady

The Stick Soldiers

Poems by

Hugh Martin

Foreword by Cornelius Eady

A. POULIN, JR. NEW POETS OF AMERICA SERIES, No. 35

BOA Editions, Ltd. ❦ Rochester, NY ❦ 2013

First Edition
13 14 15 16   7 6 5 4 3 2

For information about permission to reuse any material from this book please contact The
Permissions Company at www.permissionscompany.com or e-mail permdude@eclipse.net.

Publications by BOA Editions, Ltd.—a not-for-profit corporation
under section 501 (c) (3) of the United States Internal Revenue
Code—are made possible with funds from a variety of sources, includ-
ing public funds from the New York State Council on the Arts, a state
agency; the Literature Program of the National Endowment for the
Arts; the County of Monroe, NY; the Lannan Foundation for support
of the Lannan Translations Selection Series; the Mary S. Mulligan
Charitable Trust; the Rochester Area Community Foundation; the
Arts & Cultural Council for Greater Rochester; the Steeple-Jack
Fund; the Ames-Amzalak Memorial Trust in memory of Henry Ames, Semon Amzalak and
Dan Amzalak; and contributions from many individuals nationwide. See Colophon on page
104 for special individual acknowledgments.

ART WORKS.
arts.gov

State of the Arts

NYSCA

Cover Design: Sandy Knight
Interior Design and Composition: Richard Foerster
Manufacturing: McNaughton & Gunn
BOA Logo: Mirko

Library of Congress Cataloging-in-Publication Data

Martin, Hugh, 1984–
[Poems]
The stick soldiers : stories / by Hugh Martin — First edition.
    pages cm
Poems.
ISBN 978-1-938160-06-6 (pbk.) — ISBN 978-1-938160-07-3 (Ebook)
I. Title.
PS3613.A7788S75 2013
811'.6—dc23
                      2012044331

BOA Editions, Ltd.
250 North Goodman Street, Suite 306
Rochester, NY 14607
www.boaeditions.org
A. Poulin, Jr., Founder (1938–1996)

Contents

Foreword

. . . a doctor told us
not to disturb the scab

that needed to grow . . .
—Hugh Martin, "Full Moon, M2 Machine Gun"

Wars haunt us. Whether you win or lose, whether you wind up wounded or whole, if your house is rubble-swept or blessed, we carry the shit we do to each other in the name of one damn thing or other: Gods, land, resources, homeland security. Whatever. The ways and means are interchangeable, but the ghosts and the societal hangover linger for years, even generations, and the wounds aren't always as obvious as an exploded IED.

Walt Whitman, another poet informed by the effects of battle once wrote, "He who touches this book touches a Man." I would amend that slightly to say the reader who enters Hugh Martin's remarkable first book *The Stick Soldiers* touches a soldier, touches a war, touches the landscapes of two loaded cultures, a landscape where night-vision goggles and Kurdish lutes coexist in the same space, where laptop porn glows under the door of the base shit-house, where even a drive on a snowy stateside road can evoke the bombs that are not under the tires.

Here's eleven months worth of sawdust and sweat, dear reader. Somehow, Hugh Martin has wrung poetry from a scab, and now, the full shock and beauty and mystery of the things of war that won't let go will stick to you.

—Cornelius Eady

He could not accept with assurance an omen that he was about to mingle in one of those great affairs of the earth.

—Stephen Crane

M-16A2 Assault Rifle

Some days I clean the rifle so it shines,
a cold slice of darkness in grease-stained hands.
Some days, I hate to take it outside, dust
blowing faster, eating the morning brown.
Some days, after the warm silhouettes bow
across the green field of the firing range,
I sit against sandbags, sweat in sunlight,
and hold that grip, the muzzle's edge resting
across the top of my thigh. And some days,
when I've cleaned it for hours, I want only
to take it home for the space of blue wall
above the mantel, because it'd be wrong
to shoot again, to smear and smudge with whorls,
to blemish a thing that makes the night blush.

I.

Spring in Jalula

1.

The air is exhaust smoke, desert heat, the black
sewage-streams that don't dry.

Cows graze beside the river of shit; their noses sift
through soggy trash.

2.

Last year, the liquor store was hit with two RPGs;
today, the store is a pile of brick.

When buying a car, it is cheaper
to buy the one with bullet holes.

3.

Mohammad, the ten-year-old who doesn't go to school,
sells everything; when you hand him 300 dinars, he runs

through the streets, returns with Pepsi, chicken,
falafel. *Zam-zam?* he asks. *DVD, freaky-freaky? Knife?*

4.

After weddings, the people fill the sky
with red tracers fired from Kalashnikovs;

the tracers pass through darkness, but somewhere,
they fall back to Iraq.

5.

There is always a new bomb. Each week,
someone finds one, hidden

beneath bricks, buried beside curbs. At dusk,
people burn trash by the river. The smoke: white and blue.

6.

Daud, the town bum, walks the streets barefoot;
the cuts on his toes never heal. When he sleeps

on the same piece of cardboard beside the vendor stands,
all night he yells in broken English,

but no one ever knows what he's saying.

The Stick Soldiers

To soldiers, I hope the war is fine.
—Girl Scout Troop 472

The children have colored the cards,
dated from December,
with Christmas trees, piles of presents,
snowmen smiling, waving. Sara wants
a doll. Evan, a dog. Kyle promises
to pray for us.

Outside the hooch, we open mail,
hundreds of letters
from youth groups, scout troops,
classes of school children.

Kearns wants to write back,
ask for pictures
of older sisters.

We tape our favorites to the door.
In blue crayon, a stick-figure soldier poses
as he's about to toss
a black ball,
fuse burning,
at three other stick figures,
red cloth wrapped over faces,
Iraki written
across stick chests.

In Jalula, the children draw us pictures, too.

In white chalk, on concrete walls,
a box-shaped Humvee with two antennae

rising like balloons from the hatch.
A stick soldier holds a machine gun;
he waves at us,
us, in the Humvees.

Further down the wall, a stick man holds
an RPG
aimed toward the Humvee,
the waving soldier's head—
what the children want for Christmas,
or what they just want.

The Global War on Terrorism

Well, it just says you're being mobilized in support of the Global War on Terrorism.

—Sergeant First Class Miracle reading the mobilization order.

We stir shit in rusty cans and watch the wind
blow the flames. When we leave our desert
uniforms hanging out to dry,
the next morning

they stand on their own, inhabited by ghosts
and sand. My face, neck and hands
are tanned
to a dark, sexy red. No one wants guard duty
at Tower Nine
beside the garbage pit. The SF guys

killed a bunch of dogs
and threw them in there one day. I saw flies
all over their faces.

When Werthman's in the port-o-john
and the cracks light up blue
from his laptop, we know
what's going on.

I took a picture of a tree, the only one
on base.
When we peel our socks off, our leg hairs stick
like leeches to the skin.
No one wants to play basketball

because they can't breathe.
They have volleyball tournaments
and I play reluctantly. Hair on my neck
sometimes curls,
grows inwards, and I bleed

when I shave. I avoid First Sergeant,
because he's always checking our faces,
looking for stubble.

The Jalula Market

On long foot patrols we wanted the chickens,
roasted and bronzed, hanging

from the steel roofs of vendor stands,
the Iraqi sun burning
like a heat lamp. We had seen months

of Cobra cooking: teriyaki chicken
the color of transmission fluid; mixed vegetables

that broke like Styrofoam
in the mouth; the mush of grits
always cold. This changed, for a day, when LT Stanton—

a man who once suffered
a week of the shits

after eating vanilla ice cream
from little Mohammad,
the ten-year-old town salesman—

walked to the vendor with two Iraqi Police
and pointed to the first chicken in the row

glowing with warm grease, almost as large
as Stanton's tan bald head. The IPs sat
at a white table behind the stand; LT joined them,

setting his M4 like a twig between his knees,
the muzzle face-down

on the black asphalt. I turned my back
with the rest of the platoon, all of us a circle—
security—around the table,

the hanging chickens. Sometimes you are certain
something terrible is about
to happen, but we just watched the endless

movement of the crowd, the glares
from older men, the women passing

as if we were only date palms. LT yelled
my name. I took three steps back, turned, he handed me
a piece of the chicken wrapped

in warm pita. Not wanting anyone to see me
without both hands on the rifle, my head scanning

each detail of the crowd, I pretended
to wipe the sweat
from my temple, my cheek, but instead stuffed

the food in my mouth: tomato, onion, something
I couldn't name. On that street

some bombs had blown so close
our legs and hands shook
for hours; weeks ago, three IPs had been shot

dead in their jeep. But I just stood there
and chewed, because that chicken

was the best thing I'd tasted
in years, and somehow
I was enjoying this day—

though that wasn't something
I was supposed to show,

so I bit my tongue,
and made sure not one
person in those crowds could know.

Responding to an Explosion in Qarah Tappah

A boy's father builds IEDs in a dark corner of the family courtyard. One night, the eleven-year-old explores his father's work: he curls a det cord in small hands, rubs the smooth body of the blue mortar, feels a cold firing pin, gazes at the array of cellular phones. He touches something the wrong way, a round explodes, the boy—all over the courtyard. Second platoon hears the explosion; they drive toward the sound. When the father comes home, they blindfold him, zip-tie his hands behind his back, take him away. We drive through the empty hills, the ground so hard, so stale, it crunches under our tires as if made of sun-dried bones. We have come to assess what is left: the remaining shells, the pieces of phone, the coils of wire. We don't speak to anyone, not even each other. As we walk through the courtyard, behind three old women in black abayas, we see two small girls in flowing, flowery dresses, the hems swaying against their feet. The girls cry softly, moderately, like sorrow was something they were trying for the first time.

First Engagement

You run with the others over gravel, looking up
at the dirt-berm wall that surrounds your home, FOB Cobra,
and you climb to the edge that ends against sky.
You push with boots, claw the loose dirt with one hand,
hold the rifle in the other as the terse pops

of warning shots go silent. At berm's edge,
beneath the crooked Kevlar cover, you peek to see
the hundreds of meters of mortar-beaten
land and then why you're there: a white truck moves
down the broken asphalt road, orange sparks,

hundreds, splash from its tailgate—a vehicle-born
IED. It could be headed to the village, just north;
it could be headed for the main gate.
Inside the truck, the driver can't see
or does not see or doesn't care to see:

you, the dozens of rifles, the Bradley's black
cannon aimed to the windshield, the hood,
his own head, his passenger's head.
You steady your rifle
atop the berm, and first, the Bradley fires,

its orange tracers, almost gentle, weightless
as they fly to meet the truck's grill; the platoon follows:
down the line, they fire together. You aim. Your first shot.
But the truck slows. When you adjust, your foot slips,
you fall below the edge, unable to see. A lieutenant yells

Cease fire—silence. So this is it?
No one knows the man
was dragging rebar from the back of his truck;
no one knows he was taking it to rebuild his home;
no one knows his son, the passenger, is shot in the arm;

no one knows the man is shot in the leg, the stomach.
All you know: an hour ago, three mortars fell
from the sky for you, this vehicle with sparks
is for you, it's only day three and how many more
until you can go. Steam rises

from the hood, the blown tires sag to the concrete,
the rusted bumper hangs beneath shattered headlights,
and from the space where a door used to be,
the man falls to the road for you, for the Bradley,
for all the men, to show just how you've done.

II.

Nights in the Quadrilateral Pool of Sawdust and Sweat

—Fort Knox

In the dim room of blue tile,
the twelve steel heads spray
too hard, and the two drains choke
from too much water. We're nude

except for the rubber flip-flops
to keep fungus
from between our toes. After months, we know

each body:
the red check-mark scar
where Shotwell's appendix was lifted;
a topography
of burnt skin on Melvin's back;

Shelton's ebony penis
uncircumcised, how he'd walk the halls after,
wringing it out like a cloth, not caring
who saw; McCall's muscular symmetry
from a life of afternoons
at the World Gym in Rapid City, South Dakota;

half of Psalm 27
tattooed in Olde English
on Garcia's wide thigh, *you will*
protect me just above the kneecap; freckles

on Halpin's arms, his back (Derden, with a pen
one day asking, *can I play*
connect-the-dots); the stretch-marks,

a beet red on Leal's lower stomach;
the brown birthmark
above Kitt's left nipple; Parson, from Boston,
his strict tradition:

brown towel around his waist,
he'd walk to the rusted
industrial fan, open
the cloth with both hands

like parting a curtain for sunlight,
and he'd rock left and right
while the wind dried his balls; Wade's body
hairless and thin—we'd watched him

use those arms
wrapped in fat veins
to pop a zit
in the middle of Thome's back;
the blood streamed down
like a dash of watercolor.

The Summer of Crawling

—*Fort Knox, Kentucky, July 2002*

We low-crawl across the yellow
grass of the practice grenade-range:
sixty boys, arms and legs, holding

hard to the earth. Drill Sergeant Barnes yells,
*We're getting ready to invade Iraq
and Saddam Hussein wants you dead.*

He throws a smoke-grenade: a mist of red
floats above our bald, sun-burnt heads.
The smoke means *crawl*. Faster.

Barnes yells, *All of you will go. Half of you
will come home horizontal.* I study
a small dandelion-weed inches from my face,

spit the taste of canister-smoke
onto one of the leaves. Barnes tosses another:
a white cloud grows above the ground. We crawl,

groan, reach, our bodies sop the dirt
with sweat. When he lets us stand
in formation and march down the asphalt road

to the bayonet-assault-course, he makes us chant—
our shouts billowing against the miles of forest
at Knox—*gotta train, gotta train, gotta train to kill Hussein* . . .

The Range

We shoot green silhouettes
of men. Their blank faces

are painted beige, their plastic
chests checkered with holes,

but still, they rise in the July sunlight
like a boy too stupid to know

when to stay down, when to quit.
Drill Sergeant Grant paces

the gravel walk. He stops
to lie beside me on the beaten grass.

Between shots in the deep hush
of smoke, he says *breathe, breathe* . . .

as we watch the targets fall
flat to the earth. I never

speak, but only fire, study
the range for the next one—

hold my breath, tap
the trigger, take them down,

one by one, like it was all
the world needed done.

Basic Training

We're mopping the bays when Watson walks off and shuts himself in his locker to sleep. Watson was a guy that everyone hated but no one would fight because we all agreed he'd be like the Monty Python knight who'd come after you even when all his limbs were chopped off. On his 6'5" frame was a head like a bowling ball and when he talked—he never shut up—he always had a smile on his face that said *Fuck you*. Everyone was tired of hearing about all his girlfriends in Reno, Nevada, and all the times he'd beaten someone's ass in Reno, Nevada, so when we heard him snoring, his ass on the wooden chest of drawers, his back against the corner of the locker, Gottner walked in and clicked the combination lock, then spun the dial. Running the mop across the linoleum floor, Michaels said, *How the hell we supposed to get him out?* Gottner, from Texas, didn't look up but kept turning his mop and pushing the wringer, *The fuck should I know. He can call Reno, Nevada.* Drill Sergeant Grant was walking down the hallway with Popeye's Chicken—he always ate in front of us—and as he came in the door, Gottner yelled, *At ease* and we all stopped, stood at parade rest. Grant sipped from his drink for a few seconds and said *This Cherry Coke is good, my, so good,* and sipped again. As we stood there holding mops and brooms, staring at Grant, there was a gargled snore that came from the bay across the hall. Grant looked up, *What motherfucker is that?* With drink and bag in hand, he walked to the other bay and we followed. He didn't even speak, but just stood by the locker, nodded toward the doorway, and we understood what he wanted: six of us held the locker as three others slowly tilted it. As it reached ninety-degrees, Watson's body fell against the door and his snoring turned to *Fuck, what—*. He pounded on the door, *Open up you fucks, open up you fucks, don't fuck with me*—Grant cut him off, *Hi, Watson.* Watson went silent. Eight of us carried the locker out the front door and set it where Grant pointed, on the sidewalk beneath a small beech tree. He told us to make up our own knock-knock jokes and try them out on Watson. At night, when we thought he'd want us to get him out, Grant had us lay the locker on its backside against the concrete. All through the evening, Watson yelled and banged against the door, but after a few hours, we only heard his moans, and then nothing.

Full Moon, M2 Machine Gun

—Fort Bragg, December 2003

The night sky washes through skeletons
of trees. In the truck below, four men sleep
    sitting up, breaths of silver steam. Tonight,
    in this Carolina forest

        before we go to war, we stay awake,
        stay cold, and watch for the threats
        of nothing.

Yesterday, Captain said
    they found Saddam
        in a hole.

        Everyone says
        things will get better. Mom wrote

        Maybe you won't have to go.
    I wrote, *Yes, maybe*—but I know better.
        Beyond this muzzle,
        the white pines stand defiant; they say
            to the cold, *Fuck you;* they say it
            to the stars, too.

We remember
    Saddam's sons,
    their misshapen faces
    on the TV screen
as we stood in line
    after smallpox shots

inside the Medical Center; we clapped, yelled,
  and a doctor told us
    not to disturb the scab

that needed to grow
   over the three holes
   in our shoulders.
     A desert waits.

Tomorrow, We Go Up North

—Camp Udairi, Kuwait

Night before we cross the border
some of the guys stand outside the tent
and drink non-alcoholic beer.
I crack one and take a sip—it tastes

like shit, but I drink half
just to stand with everyone else. The beer
reminds us the desert we stand on is real,
that tomorrow we will place the bullets

into the chambers of our weapons. Never
would any of us drink non-alcoholic beer,
except for tonight. Thomas, the tall medic,
bought the fake booze at the PX

and as someone walks in
or out of the tent, he pulls a wet,
dripping can from the bucket of ice
and says their name and

you want a cold one?
No one says anything
except if they called their wives
or kids on the satellite phone. I called home—

no one picked up—told the answering machine
I was leaving in a couple weeks, a lie
for operations security. "OPSEC,"
the captain yelled all night.

I dump the other half of the beer
behind the tent and walk past Davis
and Benson who are betting
on how many miles it will be

before we get attacked. Inside,
everyone still packs
their duffel bags and rucksacks,
stuffing them until they bulge.

Four-Letter Word

I don't wanna hear that fuckin' four-letter word.
—A soldier in a bar in Leesville, Louisiana, after
getting his 35th tattoo

1.

At Fort Polk, Louisiana,
the Opposition Force shoots
all three of us,
but we enjoy this death,

which gives us a chance to sit,
smoke, rest our feet. Dying
is part of training
for war in Iraq.

We leave in two months.

2.

My Aunt Joan hates that I'm going.
She talks

at the retirement home,
My nephew is going
to EAR-RACK!
saying the four-letter word

like trying to spit food
from her mouth.

3.

Killed
when his convoy vehicle
struck a roadside bomb

Killed
when a roadside bomb
hit his vehicle on a mounted patrol

Killed
when his unit was ambushed
with small-arms fire

Killed—

4.

On the slow computer
in the Internet and Phone Center, I say
the names of the dead.

Age, hometown,
cause of death.

IED, RPG,
small arms,
car bomb—
things to be avoided.

5.

Home for Christmas leave.

This is our son, he's going to Iraq.
He's leaving for Iraq.
His unit is being mobilized for Iraq.

He has to go to Iraq.
I'll get you a drink, you're going to Iraq.
E-mail me when you get to Iraq.

Hopefully things will get better when you get to Iraq.
Are you scared about going to Iraq?
Did you know you would have to go to Iraq?

I can't imagine going to Iraq.
Is there a chance you might not go to Iraq?
Where will you be in Iraq?

What will you be doing in Iraq?
How long will you be in Iraq?
Iraq? Really? Iraq?

6.

My Chemistry professor asks
why I'm withdrawing from class.

She says, *E-mail your address,*
I'll send you guys cookies.

7.

At Ohio State
with Jake and Larry, we walk

from house to house,
keg to keg, drink beers

from a book bag. When I wake
on white carpet in a living room,
I'm not sure what has happened,

but I'm still going to Iraq.

8.

Channels went home for Christmas;
he never came back to Bragg.

He's AWOL; LT says
the Marshals will find him
within a week.

9.

Asleep in the barracks.
Three A.M., two feet
hit the floor. Someone runs

(tomorrow we will know it was Spencer)
to the lighted latrine,
and three paces from my bunk,
spew lashes

across the red floor as if dumped
from a bucket above—but he doesn't stop,
vomit falling as he runs,

and in the stall,
after coughing up the rest,
a slow breathing,
cold water in the sink; he sucks it

from a cupped hand, again and again.

10.

At the high school football game,
Dan and John shake my hand. They stand

in thick, unzipped jackets.
When we lean left

with the hundreds of heads

watching the ball in the air
soaring to our home end zone,

I feel the tremors in my chest,
the silent crowd inhaling to explode,

the open mouths,
the arms, the screams.

III.

Observation Post

Hanley spits strings of saliva-
laced dip into the gravel. Hours ago, a dud dropped
on the south side of the FOB, sent up a breath
of dust. Marwan, the interpreter,

drives to the entrance gate,
picks up his two boys. Their summer job:
filling sandbags for dinars.
At the intersection one mile down the road,
a three-round burst,
a precise incision
through the windshield. Neck, mouth, nose.

We drive with the captain in a Humvee
and find the two boys
crouched together, hands
over heads on the floor, their father
wet on their bodies.

Captain takes a photo, and we lean
toward the backseat window, as he points
at red scraps of Marwan,
beside the seatbelt buckle. Later,
he'll show everyone, magnifying
the camera's screen, *that's skull*
right there, that's skull,
as if needing others to agree.

We watch crowds carry the wood coffin
through Sadiyah's streets.
Peshmerga arrive in jeeps

with RPGs, Kalashnikovs;
they drag suspects
to the police station,
where they'll take turns
with the rifle butting.

I'm cleaning my fingernails with a Gerber;
Hanley whispers,
A shooting star. When I look, he says,
Go fuck yourself. Before dawn,
we see movement
in the retreating darkness. Through the binos:
a donkey mounts another in a field.
When our relief shows up, we say,
if you're bored, two donkeys
are fucking at three o'clock;
a dud hit before midnight;
Marwan is dead.

Raid

A dozen thin dogs bark
and follow us as we walk
the paths of the village.

Derron wants to shoot, holds his muzzle
inches from a wet nose.
I swing at one with the shovel—it jumps back,
circles our squad.

Sheikh Sharif greets us like guests,
offers chai, shakes hands.
Face covered with green cloth,
the informant points to the layers of compost, straw.

Wolfe swings the metal detector;
I dig, open the ground, toss dirt
with orange peels,
blackened tomatoes. Sergeant Kenson
stabs a shovel straight
to the split earth,
feels for steel crates.

After an hour, our necks stain from sunlight.
The dogs pace in the dust.

The Sheikh smiles,
holds his infant son,
says, *Mister, nothing,*
nods to the upturned ground.
He kisses the child, hums a song.

When LT wants to leave, I give the ground
some final stabs, kick the dirt
over upturned dirt, then stand
in the never-dead sun,
and all that's left:
a deep hole of nothing,
the dogs circling with dry tongues.

Nocturne, Traffic Control Point

In armor, sweat, and skin, I sat
in the Humvee's shell of steel.
Miles of traffic moved down the freeway,

north to Baghdad, engines shaking,
vehicles blurring against
pavement-heat ghosts.

A white car curved left, leapt the curb,
and came at us like the line of a bullet.
Jenkins traversed the 240, there were shouts

and shots—then I hovered high
above the roaring earth
on an orange bed of smoke

when the man's body, gone at the torso,
twisted toward me, flailing out
his thin, dead arm, like he wanted
to hold my hand.

Friday Night, FOB Cobra

1.

Smith, shirtless, curls forty-pound
dumbbells, veins burst

like worms over his biceps. The curls
are part of his plan for home:

a sex life.

2.

On burn detail, Ritchey stirs shit
with a metal rod,

asks Carter—standing back with a smoke—
Doesn't it make you hungry?

3.

In Tower Ten, Stevens discusses mutual funds,
interest rates. He says a young guy like me

might spend all his money on a bike, a truck,
a house. He's taking his wife

for a cruise, investing the rest,
and that's what you do with money.

4.

Jones's brother sent him a twelve-pack
of UltraSensitive LifeStyle

condoms. The box reads:
almost like wearing

nothing at all. He cuts it out,
tapes it to the front of his flak vest.

5.

When asked why his hands are so hairy,
Kenson says, with a cup of coffee in one of them

and a ball of wet Copenhagen
bulging beneath his lip, *I ain't a fuckin' girl.*

He sips four pots a day, changes the grinds
once a week. The coffee tastes of steam and heat.

6.

Kellerman's wife divorced him over e-mail.

7.

Ski boils water in a canteen cup, adds Ramen,
slices of expired Slim Jims. He discusses

the meaty juices, how the heat pulls them
for flavor. He says this meal is sacred.

8.

Sergeant Thompson has been in so many fights,
there is no cartilage left in his nose.

In line for the phone, he shows us:
bending it like an ear

with one finger, flat against his cheek.

9.

On marriage, Perry says, *It ain't like that.*
You think you just walk in the door,

and she hands you a beer,
gives you a blow job.

It ain't like that, he says. *Just wait,*
it ain't like that.

10.

Sprinkling hot sauce over cold, boiled potatoes,
Dempson talks about reading the paper,

the names of the dead. All of us know
he's slept with ninety-seven women.

After we finish our food,
he tells us about one.

Pictures of the War

When I send home a disposable camera, so my parents can develop the film, see pictures of the war, I don't know that Ellis stole it and photographed his penis. Giggling with a wad of dip nudged behind his lip, he tells me weeks after I send it, how, sitting on his bunk, he'd simply pulled up his black boxers, pointed into the darkness, and clicked. I imagine my mother taking the glossy photos from the envelope as she walks out of the store. Since I'd already taken up half the roll on the drive from Kuwait, Ellis's picture was somewhere in the middle. Most likely, she'd thumb through that section and see: row of mud homes; children shouting for candy; rusty T-72 tank; penis. The question was whether or not she'd recognize it. She might think: her son is with a bunch of men in the desert, the penis, a part of some joke, and move to the next photo. Or maybe she'd slowly flip through the pictures, study each one, thinking, *My son is at war, this is what he sees*, and, upon gazing at the close-up of the penis, think only how it reminds her of a penis, and then scold herself for such thoughts. She might just stand there, squint, move in closer, and after a few seconds become fearful, presuming it was the blurry result of a camel in the desert darkness.

After Curfew

—Jalula Police Station

A black dog sniffs the bag of smashed tomatoes
beneath the blinking lamppost.
Daud, the bum with bandaged feet,
snores face-down on a piece of cardboard
beside the concertina wire that catches trash.
There hasn't been a gunshot all night.
Inside, the drunk we put in the jail cell
vomits into a bucket. The police don't speak English,
so we smile, give the thumbs-up, and say *good*
as they point at our machine guns, flashlights,
Night-Vision, and other equipment
they don't have. When there's nothing left to point at,
two of them open the doors of a Nissan jeep,
turn up the radio's volume.
A Kurdish lute scratches
over a man's singing voice, his pitch
somewhere between a cry and a scream.
Next to the black streams, under a lamp like a spotlight,
three police, slowly, begin to dance. They lip-sync
through cigarettes, blow breaths of smoke at the sky,
hold their loaded Kalashnikovs
against their bodies, a hand on the butt,
a hand on the muzzle, and their feet shuffle,
their heads roll in slow circles;
they follow the rifle's lead.

The Rocket

Blue as the pale sky this rocket
lay beside a dry wadi
alone where there was nothing
for miles, as if a man, too tired
to take it any further
had set it here years ago, this spot
on the sun-hardened ground.
There was no wind. There was no one
but us, our trucks parked
at the edge of the valley. Sergeant Sumey,
tired of staring, walked to the rocket.
We all knew better than to touch
a thing like this, but all of us, all our hands,
had done it many times before. Sumey grabbed
the rocket like a handle to the earth,
lifted it—no longer than his M-4—
above his shoulder, and leaned back,
widened his stance, as if about to throw it
to the barren hills in the east,
so we could watch its arc, its twirl,
as if doing the rocket the favor
of making sure it left the world in pieces.

Causeway Overwatch

—As Sa'Diyah

In the predawn darkness, a white
truck speeds across the causeway,

one headlight dim. We wait in a ditch
beside the water. With hands and boots, I climb

to the concrete, stand over the faded
yellow line, flash a light above my head,

wave arms, flash again. The truck still
speeds, brights growing in the darkness.

Moving to the road's edge, I steady
the rifle to the windshield's black.

Thompson fires warning shots, two tracers,
orange in the sky. Two hundred meters.

The truck could be full of bananas, melons,
nothing—but it will not stop,

and we can shoot, all of us can shoot.
Thompson yells he will, but the lights

die, brakes wake the night, two men fall
from each side door, hands over their heads.

They crawl on their knees, the driver shouting,
I am sorry, I am sorry. He bows to the ground,

Please, please . . . My muzzle is in front
of his face. We tell him to stand, but he shakes

so much he can't. In the dark, his body
resembles another silhouette

trembling in the wind on a firing range.
Beside me, another cigarette burns,

another soldier waits to shoot, another morning
where we greet men with rifles.

Desert Nocturne

When we wake to the rotors at dawn,
I run outside shirtless with Walter,

bare feet on gravel, and try to save
the wet underwear and socks we'd left

to dry on the line. It's too late. The dust
coats all of the clothes. We squint

in sand, wind, take what we can in our arms.
Over the hills and then above: the sky

a bruised blue, the thinning moon,
the green Black Hawk sunrise.

IV.

The War Was Good, Thank You

—In the college cafeteria, a freshman girl asks, So, how was
the war?

1.

We live in small steel hooches
shaped like boxcars. We fill bags

with sand and sweat
to pile beside us. Our rifles collect dust

when we sleep. Our rifles collect dust
when we fire them.

2.

In Jalula, I stood in the turret, hands
on the Fifty. I looked over mud walls and fences

into backyards, alleyways. A man
and a woman backed from a doorway; I watched them

through dark sunglasses and the sight aperture.
They kissed, then turned—they saw me. The man smiled,

as if wanting me to keep it a secret. I didn't tell anyone.

3.

Some afternoons, I lay outside shirtless
and set ice cubes

on my closed eyelids. I let them melt.

4.

After weddings, people point rifles
to the sky, and fire,

as if wanting to put holes
through heaven.

5.

Groups send care packages. There's always so much
ChapStick, baby wipes; we pile it in boxes

or throw it to the children. I spoil myself
with ChapStick, balm my lips

even when it's not needed. Outside the wire,
I raise my chin to the sun, flex

my lips, kiss them together, not afraid
of anything, not afraid at all.

Demobilization

On Bain's 23rd we fill a piñata
with cigars and small

sample bottles of liquor.
When the red donkey's body

breaks, falls in two pieces,
Bain keeps beating it against the grass.

Home from Iraq, Barking Spider Tavern

—Cleveland, Ohio

Outside on the smoker's patio,
the Army vet shakes my hand
for the twentieth time, yells
about *loyalty, country, duty.*

Between gulps, he explains his shame
for missing the Storm—
a bum knee, ten thousand
beers later, and now, another war
to miss. We finish the cans,
throw them at a wall, crack new ones.

The summer sweat sticks to his face
and in his eyes is the horror
of not going, that he'd live
all his life having to say *no,*
blaming a bum knee,
hitting it hard with a palm
to punish it.

He shakes my hand again,
grabs my shoulder,
and then seems to want to kiss me,
suck out whatever was left
since he wanted to taste it so badly.

Barracks Dream

On a blue blanket in a wide Ohio field,
he wants to wrap his arm around her shoulders.
The white pines are warm beside them.
The men far away check cords
that will send detonations
through the summer darkness, but the waiting
only reminds him of Tower Nine with Daley—
their fight on the twelve to four shift,
shouting long after midnight, why or why not
the war was just, waiting for the never-
accurate mortars to fall out of the sky. They came close
to blows, and Daley left the post,
stood alone by the berm, but both of them knew
they needed to feel
a fist on their faces, so much inside
trying to explode: the people, the shit-streams,
the electricity from the blasts. Daley punched
a sandbag instead. They waited
the final hours in silence. Now,
he lies beside this girl.
After all the months, the mornings
with men, the barracks dreams,
he can't lift his hand
just to touch her.

Firework Elegy

Inside an olive sky,
they huddled on quilts
stretched over hills.

They'd come to watch the bright
splashes thrown at the sky,
the ways of speaking—light, spark, rise.

He hated that this was home.

They shouted
to each blast, dressed
their children
with fire and flags.

He clutched grass from the ground,
but soon let go,
let his body touch the earth.
His hands shook.

The colors continued to sound
and he covered his face with a forearm.

From the sky,
it's a wonderful war:
tracer round reds,
blooming explosions,
and all our cigarettes,
one for every dying star.

First Snow

I'm driving on a road that will not explode.
Out the window, stiff white pines
huddle above the wall of limestone
torn with dynamite
to make space
for the three lanes of 77 North.

Trash is still suspicious.
A bag. A bottle. A bump
in the gravel. Torn patches
of iced grass.

I used to dream of men with shovels.
Thousands digging
beside the long Iraq road,
smiling with triangular teeth
chiseled from shrapnel
jut from wine-red gums.

They sow the soil with bombs,
or what we name:
Improvised Explosive Device.

*

Although there is a hole
in this roof, Spoonman doesn't
sit on a strap, body not
half out in the open air, cigarette not
on lips, machine gun not mounted, not
held in his greasy hands not there.

*

I've left college to drive home
for Thanksgiving. The first flakes of snow
touch—flail—across the windshield,
fade behind on the black concrete.
As I push the switch, the sunroof slides
to let in the wind, the snow,
and who can say about loving—
when we put holes in our roofs for the sky—
that we don't, and we can't.

V.

Doc's Kill

In the police parking lot
we chase a dog
that's limped for days
after a hit from a car.

We'd seen the stretches
of red skin sweat
where black fur was torn away, and finally,
Doc said,
he'd put it out of its misery.

We cornered the mutt
against Hesco barriers
that brimmed with Iraq's dirt.

The dog stood, shaking for balance,
and Doc stepped forward,
pointed the barrel to the head, fired,
and as the dog jumped back, the bullet

pierced the lower jaw like a hole punch.
It ran off, limping every third step,
shrieking from its gut.
With rifle pointed, Doc chased after,
but there were too many trucks,
soldiers—no clear shot.

The dog weaved
through garbage-laced concertina wire
and vanished into the brush. Even gone,
we heard its yelping,
constant over all the village.

Face red and wet, Doc gripped his rifle hard.
Everyone knew it wasn't his fault,
but he waited,
aimed at the foliage,
ready to show everyone
when he set out to kill something,
he meant it.

Ways of Looking at an IED

*Notice that in both photographs of the artillery shells there is a wire
leading from the bag. Also notice that the plastic bag had sand
thrown on top of it to make it look more like roadside trash.*

—1st Infantry Division Soldier's Handbook to Iraq

1.

Beside the field of potato rows,
Sumey sees an alarm clock

taped to a two-liter bottle. We create
a perimeter, back up the trucks, flatten

the potatoes under tires.
The Explosive Ordnance Disposal team

isn't sure; when they're not sure,
they blow it up.

2.

Why don't you walk over there, Spoon says,
and get yourself a Purple Heart.

3.

With a broom, a woman beats a rug
draped over a clothesline. LT waves her away. *Bomb,*

bomb, he says, but she shakes her head,
turns her hips to swing again.

4.

Spoon is awarded
the Purple Heart in June

when the shrapnel misses his head,
but the bricks that hide the bomb

knock him unconscious.

5.

When the shell detonates beside our truck,
the sound is too loud to hear; the wind wraps us

with shrapnel, bricks, smoke; the ballistic windshield
shatters; glass on Kenson's cheek—

blood like smeared lipstick.

6.

For three hours we clear the neighborhood
because of a black plastic bag.

The staff sergeant in the bomb suit
orders everyone to *back the fuck up* even farther.

In the bag he finds six ripe tomatoes.

7.

Sergeant Sumey says he almost vomits
turning in the turret

to see our truck vanish
inside smoke. *Thought you were all dead.*

8.

We avoid trash, disturbed soil, animal carcasses.
We arrest men

who dig beside the road.
We hate the ground.

9.

Outside the city: rocks stacked
like children's building blocks.

Sergeant Kenson won't wait for EOD. *It's nothing,*
he yells, and no one can stop him

when he starts to walk;
even LT tries to restrain him, but he walks,

and all four of us in the truck shout,
but it's no use. When he lifts his leg

to kick the pile,
we look down. We close our eyes.

Green Dreams

Tell me where bad men hide, young Iraqi boy.
That's why I stand here. How closely you study me from across the street
in broken sandals and dust-covered clothes. Talk to me.

Young boy. Somewhere my mother worries for me.
On this street, with my men behind me, I sometimes feel explosive.
Behind this mask, this costume, I am scared.

Listen to me. At night I dream of grass. Thick fields of glowing grass.
On that road between us, men set bombs for trucks. They set one for me.
I called my mother to say I was okay. Her voice carried from another
        dimension.

Listen. Earth is the only place to be. You know as much as me.
All we can do is be men. Just be men. All that's certain is that our bodies
will lie horizontal riding the earth's ethereal spin.

Tell me where bad men hide. I will kill them.
Study me. I am not Mister. These red hands know this rifle; so smooth,
        cozy,
I do not want to let go. Dear boy, no, not *Mister*—look at me, say, *War*.

Site 947: A Situation Report

—There are 946 suspected WMD sites in Iraq

Again we drove through the night,
the splash of black
on our tires. We found the valley
in the stale hills miles from the village
of As Sa'Diyah.

From a naked ridge, we looked down
through NVG goggles
and saw the green
swamp of shaking sticks,
thousands of legs,
arms pulsing,

falling atop each other: hundreds
of camel spiders
fucking in the moonlight. We knew

to be still. We stood
as if at attention. They moved,
a swarm on the ground,
all of them touching,
the entire swamp shifting
as they changed positions.

We backed up, our boots slow
on the sand,
but for no reason,
Jenson began to applaud.

Although they didn't seem to notice,
we jumped into the Humvees

and drove, our rear gunner scanning
from the turret, the dust

from our trucks gliding, blue
in the moonlight,
like a slow rain off the ridge.

The Burn Pit Detail at FOB Cobra

We stand in the Humvee's steel bed
and heave bags of trash
with both hands
to the wide crater below.

> We throw piles of opened
> boxes sent from our mothers,
> the USO. We push out
> the bent, rotting lumber

> left too long
> in the sun. We toss the torn
> tires of Humvees, the sandbags
> that split in half—we burn

everything, and we stand
beside the blue smoke
of our war's leftovers. After
the bed's empty,

we light cigarettes,
watch outside the wire:
three hundred meters out,
past the four rolls of concertina wire

> in a wide field of desert,
> two of the stray dogs fight.
> They jump to their hinds,
> mouths wide

for each other, but between the flashes
of burn pit smoke, they seem to be
in a dance, a moment
before a kiss, though just when their lips

could meet, the pit glows, the smoke
thickens—we can only see
their long shadows collide, fall.
At dawn, we'll send a detail

to gather the dog who lost.
With a snow shovel they'll scoop
the body into a double plastic bag.
To keep the dog

from becoming a bomb,
like everything,
they'll dump it to the flame
and ash of the pit.

This Morning, We Carry Body Bags

1.

brand-new, still sealed in plastic wrap,
pile them in the back of the truck.

The dip bulges from LT's lip and I imagine

2.

bullets against the truck
like horizontal rain.

Before dawn, four men shot
six Iraqi soldiers dead

as they slept on cots,
dragged outside the checkpoint hut

3.

because it was too hot.
At the Jalula hospital, traffic stops. Men smoke

in white dishdashas that wave
in the wind like bedsheets. From the hills,

a Black Hawk rises. We close eyes,

cover faces, not wanting to feel

4.

flying pieces of earth. Four men run
the first body to the chopper;

it bounces on the green gurney
beneath an IV bag held

by a hand to the sky.

Nocturne with Sandstorm

—Northern Kuwait, Arabian Desert

By dawn, the moon seems cut in half
with a dull razor. The soldier writes
his mother, but not of the dream
where he's lost both arms,
and tries again,
and again, to hug her.

The brown sheet moves in from the east,
and three camels wait,
black ghosts grazing
on white dunes of sand.

The curtain will cover the desert
with desert, but the men brush teeth,
lace boots, finish
cigarettes. Kuwait reminded them
of when they were boys, playing ball
on the unkempt, little league infields.

In a white pickup, a Bedouin drives with his son
away from the storm. The boy stares
out the window
at the waking men,
the line of trucks.

When the pickup passes the convoy,
the boy leans out, waves his hand wildly,
left to right.

After the soldier seals the envelope,
places it in the pocket of his ruck,

he waves back,
but the boy only sees
his lifted arm,
an open hand. The wall of dust
swallows it all.

Even as the hovering cloud
gently comes to take him too,
the boy yells
from the window—his voice nothing
over the truck's engine—*ma'a salaama, ma'a salaama.*
Goodbye, goodbye . . .

VI.

Nostos: Quinn's Bar, Cleveland Heights

—*January, 2005*

1.

The beer is flat and served in clear
plastic cups. McGuire hands the barman

a blue 250 Dinar note—a gift
from the stack I brought home. The man lifts

the paper to his face: The Great Mosque
of Samarra illuminated
by green fluorescent lights
hanging above the shelf
of liquor bottles.   *Maybe,*

McGuire says, *He'll take it.*

2.

At Bragg, we walk in desert boots
on a tarmac of ice. Five of us wait

in the engine's leftover
heat. Ten minutes
in America, our first detail:

unload the bags, the rucks, of 400 men.
A crowd waits
                    in a gymnasium

webbed with red and white streamers, blue
balloons, hand-
written signs.

3.

       Iraqi Violence Intensifies as Election Nears

       U.S. Ends Search for Weapons

       Ohio State 34, Notre Dame 14

       Largest Passenger Plane Launched in France

4.

They are happy I am home
in time for New Year's Eve dinner
at Chez Lola on the frozen
         Vermilion.

    With hands still red from the Iraqi
    sun, I spoon lobster bisque
    to my mouth, a body

    much less
         without the plated-vest, the ammo
         pouches full, overflowing.

The waiter suggests the salmon.

5.

Zimmer would say: "_____,"

if he hadn't died
in Kufa
from a young Shiite boy's
RPG. It was almost midnight

beside the Euphrates in June. I was
       three hours north, standing
       in guard post six, watching Iraq,
       waiting for the relief, so I could sleep.

6.

McGuire throws the bar a wad of ones,
hands me two cups.

Back there, I wanted to go home
and have

the whole world. Here,

the crowd smells
of cherry vodka and sleet. The room is dense

       with bodies in jackets, scarves,
       pushed to the wooden walls
           beneath a cloud of smoke.

The people shift as the place
seems to shake. Some of their smiles

are so large, it's like there was never
a war to begin with.

7.

                    The plane is seven stories high
                    and can seat 555 passengers.

8.

My father's friend says, *We know*

before you went in,
a convoy of trucks crossed
                    the Syrian border.
                    We know.

9.

We stand in the belly
of the plane,
throw green duffels

through the winter Carolina air—they slam
to the steel bed of a blue truck, dust

still stuck to the vinyl
scatters to the black night like snow.

10.

Glad you're back.
Fuck that place.

Welcome home.
We know he had weapons.

Remember the planes.
I'll get you a beer.

He helped Al-Qaeda.
Do you have to go back?

Were you scared?
You pop any A-Rabs?

11.

My father says I should have
the most expensive dish. *Anything*, he says.
        The waiter pours white wine

        into the thin bowl of glass.
        He sets a fork, a knife—
        the cloth like a skin over the table. On the plane
        home, they made us remove
        the steel firing pin

        from our Sixteens. I dropped mine like a cigarette
        inside my breast pocket, buttoning
                it shut.

12.

In Shanksville, Pennsylvania,
the only recognizable human
body part
was a piece of spinal cord—
five vertebrae attached.

13.

Whiskey falls from the brim
of a double-shot glass,
seeps down the ridges
            of my fingers.

McGuire and Valenti
order again.

        In between the darkness
        on every wall, beer signs glow.
        The green door at the entrance
opens and closes: January wind
        rushes against our faces.

One year ago, I left. They kept on
drinking. One in each hand.

        I toast
        the IEDs
        for not taking mine.

14.

Baggage Detail never gives two shits
about the bags. We throw every green

duffel, every massive ruck
with all the sleepy strength
in our bodies. We hope

      the bags hit the bed
      and crack in half. Each time my hands grasp,
           then heave,
           the gear through air, like the other men,
      I say,
      Fuck it.

      Fuck it.

15.

      The waiter lowers the dish: filet
      mignon, bleu cheese, a dash
           of mashed potatoes. He sets
           the serrated knife
               to the right of the plate, blade facing
               the steak.

I hear the wick
burning on the beige candle
at the table's middle.

      We spent a year talking
      about the food we'd eat, the drinks
      we'd drink.

Now all that's left to do is lift the knife.

16.

The children smile
as the electric train circles
the fake pine in Tom's apartment.

      I follow Tom and Jason to the bedroom.
      We'd almost finished
      a case of Labatt's. Tom lifts
      a blue bath towel
      from the top of a closet, unrolls it
      across the king-size bed.

            I put down my can.

        Tom's postdeployment gift
        to himself:
        Semi-automatic Bushmaster M4 Carbine.

            He hands it to me.

17.

      I vomit in the corner, go back to the bar.

Outside, through the frosted window,
Valenti kicks some kid's ribs
like he used to kick footballs
for St. Ed's.   *Fuck it.*

Before we join Val,
I order a round. We hold the shots high
        over the crowd. I try to toast,

        but don't know what I'm saying.

One more of these.
        Two more. Three—

18.

Tom and Jason hold the others:
                a long rifle, another M4. We nuzzle
                those black things
                against our bodies and hands. We peer

        through the sights
                trying to find
                something.

        When Tom's mother walks in
        holding three bulbs
        she wants us to hang, we turn—
        cheeks tucked to stocks, three muzzles
                                pointing.

19.

The gray clouds bulge
above the black Cleveland skyline.
        The Lake

is a frozen parade of white hills
that stretch north. McGuire holds
a silver Zippo to the night. The flame leans

horizontal with the wind.
My suede collar

is still wet with grape vodka. We walk
with small steps

    and trust the ice
    is firm enough by now. Further.

    I can hear the flakes
sticking to my cheeks.
The frozen snow
    cramps with our steps

like the deep Diyala sand
hardened by the sun,
    and ahead, like fading lights,
    the flurries tunnel forward.

Acknowledgments

Some of the poems in this collection were first published in the following journals, sometimes under different titles:

Alaska Quarterly Review: "After Curfew";

The American Poetry Review: "The Stick Soldiers," "Doc's Kill";

Another Chicago Magazine: "Nostos: Quinn's Bar, Cleveland Heights";

Blackbird: "Ways of Looking at an IED," "Site 947: A Situation Report," "The Burn Pit Detail at FOB Cobra";

Consequence: "Green Dreams";

Crazyhorse: "M-16A2 Assault Rifle";

The Kenyon Review: "Spring in Jalula";

The Kenyon Review online: "This Morning, We Carry Body Bags";

Michigan Quarterly Review: "Nights in the Quadrilateral Pool of Sawdust and Sweat," "The Range," "The Summer of Crawling," "Desert Nocturne," "First Engagement," "Barracks Dream," "Demobilization";

Mid-American Review: "The War Was Good, Thank You";

Narrative: "Traffic Control Point," "Home from Iraq, Barking Spider Tavern";

Nashville Review: "Four-Letter Word";

The New Republic: "The Jalula Market";

River Styx: "Basic Training";

Tygerburning Literary Journal: "Full Moon, M2 Machine Gun," "Pictures of the War," "Causeway Overwatch";

War, Literature & the Arts: "Responding to an Explosion in Qarah Tappah," "Raid";

Willow Springs: "Friday Night, FOB Cobra," "Observation Post."

"Firework Elegy" and "First Snow" were finalists in the 2011 Winning Writers War Poetry Contest.

"Tomorrow, We Go Up North," "The Global War on Terrorism," "The War Was Good, Thank You," and "Green Dreams" appeared in the chapbook *So,*

How Was the War?, winner of the 2008 Wick Student Chapbook Competition (Kent State UP, 2010), selected by Maggie Anderson.

"Nocturne with Sandstorm" was chosen and displayed as part of the 7th Avenue Streetscape Series in Phoenix, Arizona.

"Spring in Jalula," "Observation Post," and "Friday Night, FOB Cobra" appeared in *Remembrances of Wars Past: A War Veterans Anthology*.

A special thank you for their friendship and the time they gave in helping me form and shape this collection: Norman Dubie, Cynthia Hogue, and Sally Ball. Thank you to my friends and mentors over the years for their wisdom, support, and advice: T.R. Hummer, Jeannine Savard, Alberto Rios, Beckian Fritz-Goldberg, Brandon Davis Jennings, Jane Varley, Meghan Wynne, Whit Arnold, Todd Warhola, Meg Thompson, Fernando Pérez, John-Michael Bloomquist, Kathleen Winter, Sean Nevin, Eduardo Corral, Endre Szentkiralyi, The ZBA. Sincere appreciation for their many readings and critiques of these poems: Rachel Andoga, Dexter Booth, Shane Lake, Eman Hassan. Many thanks to my family for their continuous support and encouragement.

For their generous support, I am indebted to the following: Virginia G. Piper Center for Creative Writing for fellowships that sent me to the Prague Summer Program and the National University of Singapore. Arizona State University for a Graduate College Completion Fellowship that gave me time to complete this book. The entire staff of The Wick Poetry Center at Kent State University.

Sincere gratitude to BOA Editions Ltd., Peter Conners, and Cornelius Eady. Thank you, Benjamin Busch, for your incredible photo.

This book is dedicated to all of 3rd Platoon: Chaye, Ketchum, Derr, K-Neck, Doc Johnson, Pig Pen, Ondecker, Bell, Hall, Treen, Sumey, Lohn, Callaway, Wolfey, Fire Marshal Davis, Little Martin, Korbel, Iddings.

About the Author

Hugh Martin grew up in northeastern Ohio and served six years in the Army National Guard as an M1A1 Tanker. He deployed to Iraq in 2004 and after returning home he graduated from Muskingum University. Martin is the author of the chapbook *So, How Was the War?* (Kent State UP, 2010) and his work has appeared on *PBS Newshour*, *The New York Times'* "At War" blog, and was selected as the first winner of *The Iowa Review's* Jeff Sharlet Memorial Award for Veterans. Martin has an MFA from Arizona State University and is currently a Stegner Fellow at Stanford University.

BOA Editions, Ltd.
The A. Poulin, Jr. New Poets of America Series

Colophon

The Stick Soldiers, poems by Hugh Martin, is set in Bernhard Modern, a digital version of the font designed by the graphic artist Lucian Bernhard (1883–1972) and first cut by American Type Founders in 1937.

The publication of this book is made possible, in part, by the special support of the following individuals:

Anonymous
Susan DeWitt Davie
Anne Germanacos
Michael Hall
Robert & Willy Hursh
Keith Kearney & Debby McLean, *in memory of Peter Hursh*
X. J. & Dorothy M. Kennedy
Jack & Gail Langerak
Dorianne Laux & Joseph Millar, *in honor of Ernest Green*
Katy Lederer
Boo Poulin
Steven O. Russell & Phyllis Rifkin-Russell